www.geluck.com/en
www.facebook.com/lecatofgeluck

ISBN 978-2-930540-14-6
There is a 'Le Chat' app for iPhone/iPad and Android

WHO'S LE CAT ?

Apparently there are readers around the world who don't know who I am, or who draws me, or the name of my agent. This I find hard to believe. But I have been inundated with a flood of emails - (What...?) my agent informs me that this is a pleonasm, whatever that is (they think they're so clever, agents) - asking for more information about me. Well I say to you: "Stop asking me things which were clearly explained in the Introduction to my previous album, entitled 'Le Cat' - with, I thought, a minimalist clarity and true sense of the focused signifier !"

So I suggest you go back to that album and read the Introduction on pages 3 and 4. And if you don't have the album, then go and buy it ! (What...?) My agent informs me that it is never a good idea to piss off your readers or potential publishers in the Introduction by being arrogant and bad-tempered because they will either **a)** read no further in the bookshop and hence not buy the book or **b)** decide not to buy the rights for Papua-New Guinea, Swaziland, or wherever, thereby severely limiting the amount of commission he (the agent) will make from me.

So, reluctantly, I shall resort to the system used the world over by people wishing to know everything from luggage weight limits to the symptoms of sexually transmitted diseases ... **FAQs** !

Who is Le Cat and what is his life history ?
See album 'Le Cat' pages 3 & 4.
Who is the author and illustrator ?
Philippe Geluck, an amazingly intelligent, creative, warm, sensitive hunk of a man whose imagination knows no limits and whose contribution to world humour will be remembered for time immemorial (for more about this wonderful man see my album 'Le Cat' pages 3 & 4).
How can I publish Le Cat in Swaziland ?
See my agent.
Is it true that Le Cat is sexist, ageist, homophobic, and politically incorrect ?
See my lawyer.
Is it true that Le Cat is liberal, fluffy, and politically committed to ridding the world of all reductive "-isms" (except Revolutionary Humourism, of which he is a devoted follower) ?
See my lawyer.
(What...?)
My agent says to shut up and let the people read the book.
Enjoy your meal !

PHILIPPE GELUCK

LE CAT STRIKES BACK

Translated and adapted from the French by Alan Ward

COMICKING OUT

7

HONESTLY ! YOU'D THINK THAT A QUEEN WHO POSES
FOR A BANKNOTE WOULD HAVE THE DECENCY
TO TAKE OUT HER ROLLERS !

LIVING UNDER A DICTATORSHIP
IS NO REASON NOT TO SHARE A JOKE

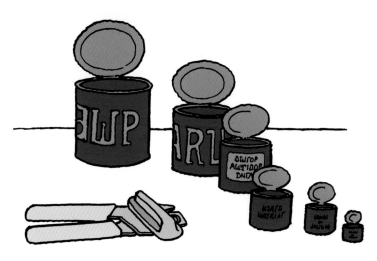

CANNED FOOD OF THE WORLD NO.54 RUSSIA

FAMOUS STATUES OF THE WORLD #29

THE MANNEKEN PIS DE MILO

FIGURE 1
NUDE STANDING

FIGURE 2
NUDE CLOTHED

11

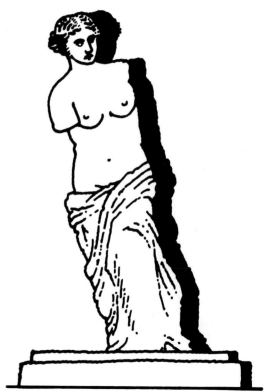

The mouse : — You ordered a takeaway.

Le Cat : — Yes, I ordered a warm meal.

The mouse : — Here it is !

Le Cat : — But I don't see anything. Where is it ?

The mouse : — It's me.

Le Cat : — Right ! Come in ...

19

NEWTON DE MiLO

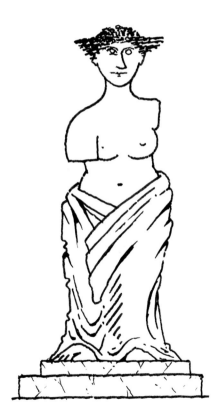

TELL DE MiLO

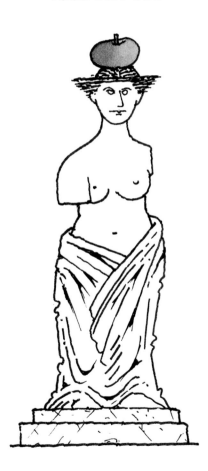

MAGRiTTE DE MiLO

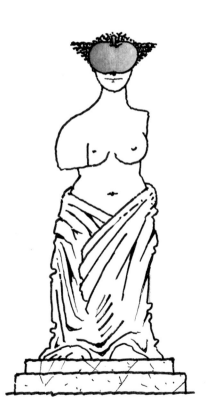

21

THE ENGLISH SENSE OF FAIR-PLAY
KNOWS NO BOUNDS

FULL-FAT YOGHURT
WITH REAL SELL-BY DATES

SHIVA BUYS HIS
UNDERARM DEODORANT

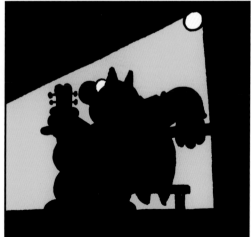

30

31

REINCARNATION EXPLAINED TO ANIMALS

EYE TEST FOR THE DEAF AND DUMB

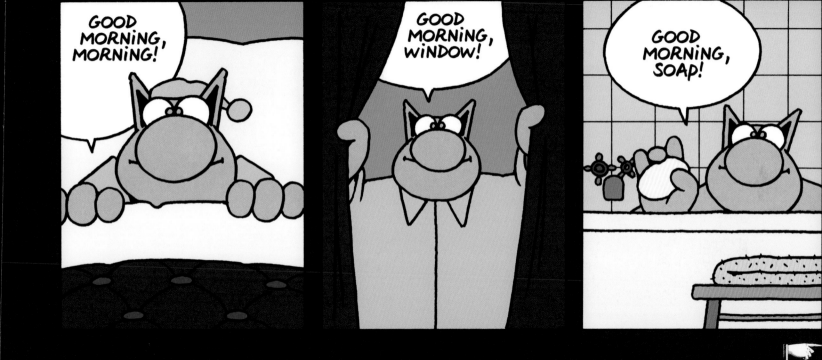

40

41

44

45

THE WORLD'S GREATEST SCRABBLE PLAYER

HE FOUND A 7-LETTER WORD IN HiS SLEEP !

210 POiNTS !

47

DON'T BEG

AND DON'T FETCH THE BALL!

YOU DON'T TALK TO A STUFFED DOG

LIKE YOU DO TO THE OTHERS

DO YOU, REX?

HAVE YOU SEEN THAT FAT SLUT? SHE'S GOT THE SAME DRESS AS ME!

TRUE! BUT SHE HASN'T GOT THE SAME SHOES

SNACK-TIME AT THE BELGIAN EMBASSY IN TOKYO

THE MYSTERIES OF ART EXPLAINED TO CHILDREN (PART 11)

YOU SEE WHAT HAPPENS IF YOU KEEP BITING YOUR NAILS

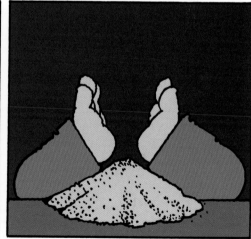

53

FROM THE GANGSTER HALL OF FAME

THE POST-iT MOB

THE COW DE MiLO
COURTESY MUSEUM OF MALMÖÖ

59

STRANGE BUT TRUE !
SiAMESE TWiNS JOiNED AT THE HAiR

CAN MOBiLES FRY YOUR BRAiN ?

DO TREES LIKE BEING CUT DOWN ?

IT ALL DEPENDS ON HOW YOU CUT THEM !

RECOGNITION AT LAST !

COMICS OFFICIALLY RECOGNISED AS A GENUINE ART FORM: THE NEW 100 FRANC NOTE TO BE ISSUED IN OCTOBER

(1) IF YOU WANT TO GET AHEAD
(2) GET A HAT

MISS WET BURKA, KABUL, 1999

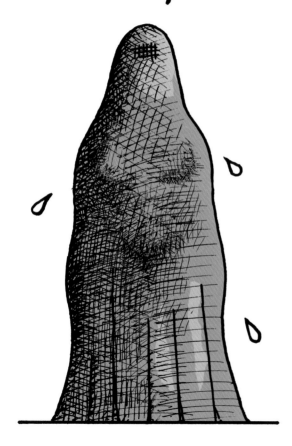

TODAY'S QUIZ
THE ARTIST HAS COPIED HIS CARTOON AND INTRODUCED A MISTAKE. CAN YOU SPOT IT?

ANSWER: THE ARTIST COPIED THE WRONG CARTOON

VENUS DE MILO (AGE 4)

71

73

VEGETARIAN CHRISTMAS
WE TRY TO CATER FOR ALL CONVICTIONS

THE DONKEY AND THE OX HAVE BEEN
REPLACED BY AN ONION AND A TURNIP

COOL !

A PACIFIST GIVING
HIS SON A BIRTHDAY PRESENT...
TIN CONSCIENTIOUS OBJECTORS

82

84

85

DARWINISM FOR DUMMIES
WHICH OF THESE IS THE BEST EXAMPLE OF NATURAL SELECTION?

NO.1   NO.2

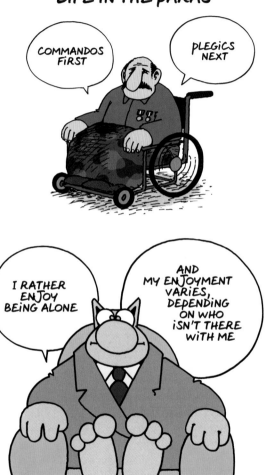

88

THE INVISIBLE MAN'S WIFE LOSES HER TEMPER

RODIN'S THE THINKER DE MILO

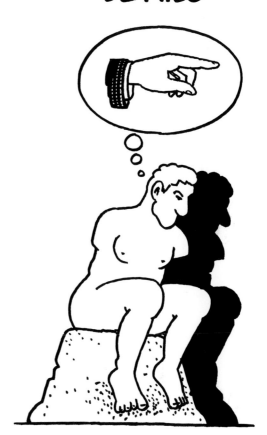